BONE-SONGS AND SANCTUARIES

BONE-SONGS AND SANCTUARIES

New and Selected Poems

Michael Jennings

The Sheep Meadow Press
Riverdale-on-Hudson, New York

Copyright © 2009 by Michael Jennings

All rights reserved. No part of this publication may be reproduced or transmitted in any form or by any means, electronic or mechanical, including photocopy, recording, or any information storage and retrieval system, without permission in writing from the publisher, except in the case of brief quotations in reviews.

Designed and typeset by The Sheep Meadow Press
Cover art "Gates of Dawn" by Darryl Hughto © 2000 36x51"
Distributed by The University Press of New England

All inquiries and permission requests should be addressed to the publisher:

The Sheep Meadow Press
PO Box 1345
Riverdale, NY 10471

Library of Congress Cataloging-in-Publication Data

Jennings, Michael, 1948-
 Bone-songs and sanctuaries : new and selected poems / by Michael Jennings.
   p. cm.
 ISBN 978-1-931357-72-2
 I. Title.
 PS3560.E525B66 2009
 811'.54--dc22

                                        2009012753

For Suzanne and Shane

> *while for him,*
> *Though he bends to be blent in the prayer, how loud and above what*
> *Furious spaces of fire do the distracting devils*
> *Orgy and hosannah, under what wilderness*
> *Of black silent waters weep.*
>
> —Ted Hughes, "Thrushes"

TABLE OF CONTENTS

The Book of Losses

Before Speech	3
Squandered by the Hundred Millions	4
Crocodile	5
The Great Mother, After Long Drought	6
Beluga	7
Black Wolf at Midnight	8
Among Mushers	10
Pilgrimage	11
Photograph: Desert Canyon	13
Vilnius Glimpses	14
Reading Heaney	17
Drum Song	18
Lowell	19
Talkin' Bob's Blues	20
A Dream of Falling	23

Dream Walk

This, Of Course, Is What Money Won't Buy	27
Trees	36
March Invitation	37
The Mountain	38
Geese	39
Fog	41
Nightwood	42
Hawk	43
Solstice	44
Raccoon	45
Nightscape	46
Diffusions of August	47
At Twilight	49

Sometime Before Words Perhaps	50
Her Dalliance	51
Tiger Dance	52
Today Perhaps the Lizard	53
Always	54
Scoffers	55
October Sun	56
Ghost Moon	57
The Road Home, November	58
The Landscape of Missing You	59
A Moment in February	60
Once	61

A Dance of Stone

Ur of the Chaldees, 1958	65
Cow Skull	66
The Egg Woman	67
Hanoon	68
Along the Avenue of Dead Gestures	70
In the Bazaar, the Laying On of Hands	71
The Wind-Curved Sandhills	72
A Dance of Stone	74
Heat	77
Inner Sanctum	87
Old Mountains	89

Lamentations

Alexandra	95
Remains	109
Invocations	111
Mary	124
Lamentations	127
Ancient Music	132

Dust and a Good Wind

Six Tenant Farmers, Without Farms, Hardman County, Texas. 1938	135
Woman of the High Plains, Texas Panhandle. 1938	136
Damaged Child, Shacktown, Elm Grove, Oklahoma. 1936	137
Child and Her Mother, Wapato, Yakima Valley, Washington. 1939	139
On the Great Plains, Near Winner, South Dakota. 1938	140
Walking Wounded, Oakland. 1954	141
Grayson, San Joaquin Valley, California. 1938	143
Toquerville, Utah. 1953	145
Man Stepping From Curb. 1956	147

ACKNOWLEDGEMENTS

I would like to thank the following publishers of the several small books that contained many of the poems included here:

Heliographis: *The Hardman County Sequence* (1980)
Pine Press: *A Dance of Stone* (1984), *Ghost Moon* (1997)
Basfal Books: *Totems* (1994)
Orchises: *Silky Thefts* (2007)
Foothills Publishing: *Once* (2008)

I would also like to thank the following publications (some now defunct) where many of the poems originally appeared:

Beloit Poetry Journal: "Hawk"
Birmingham Poetry Review: "March Invitation"
Bitterroot: "Trees"
Bottomfish: "Scoffers"
The Chattahoochee Review: "Tiger Dance"
The Comstock Review: "Remains"
Corresponding Voices (an anthology by Point of Contact Productions): all poems in "Sometime Before Words"
Ekphrasis: "Six Tenant Farmers, Without Farms, Hardman County, Texas 1938"
Graham House Review: "Nightwood"
The G.W. Review: "October Sun"
The Northern Review: "Geese"
The Sewanee Review: "A Dream of Falling"
The Southern Review: "The Road Home, November"
Stone Canoe: "Black Wolf at Midnight"
Tar River Poetry: "Squandered by the Hundred Millions"
Vanderbilt Review: "Heat"
Vitruvius: "The Great Mother, After Long Drought," "Talkin' Bob's Blues," and "Vilnius Glimpses"

Yellow Medicine Review: "Among Mushers," "Pilgrimage," and "Inner Sanctum"

Thanks also to New York State for a Creative Artist Public Service (CAPS) Grant in Poetry that allowed for the completion of the poems included in "Dust and a Good Wind," and to the Rome Arts Center for their Second Prize award for "Old Mountains" in the Milton Dorfman Poetry Prize Contest in 2002.

THE BOOK OF LOSSES

BEFORE SPEECH

was the wolf pack, the moon's children,
her insignia borne in the whites of her faces.

There was high ground at the heart of their forest
sacred for long sight, steeped in their smells.

There was bow and gesture, a sniff of the ear
that meant home, that meant heart,
that meant abiding mother with her belly in the dirt.

There was signal flashed across space.
There was the will to sing.
Anyone could start

SQUANDERED BY THE HUNDRED MILLIONS

his hell-hunks of rotting flesh
left to slough from his bones
like sacrifices to the god of steel,

one and one and one
he died, she died, they all died,
their stunned unreckoning

rose into stars, numberless as stars.
And the night came
lifting him up with his black rage

and gave him back his magical curving horns,
and lifted his mountainous woolly back-skull
onto the still larger mountains of black woolly shoulders,

and polished his small black eyes
and sharp hooves, his thunderous black bones,
and patched his scraggy, reeking beard.

But by morning the tractors had come
and the grasses vanished, and the dust came,
and that was the end of the first day.

CROCODILE

Old bubble brain
floating in primordial ooze—
Turn him on his back
and he sinks into coma,
forgets yesterday, hardly fathoms
tomorrow.

How easily we condescend
in our neocortical glimpse.
He cannot laugh or be sociable.
His one purpose
to go on expanding, to eat
and be filled and eat again.

Mountain ranges grow from his back.
His each scale anticipates
the iron age by eons.
He is the Hindu calendar
written in Braille.
For him it's still the beginning of time.

Expressionless as God.
His undulant tail
the shadowy frond of some first fern
the abstract angels dance on.

THE GREAT MOTHER, AFTER LONG DROUGHT

so tiny eyed, so tired, so wrinkle-rivered
in her skin of dust,
has trudged so long in billowing skirts of dust,
knelt fat-assed and humbled as Old Mammy
in chasms of dust—
her great trumpeting trunk following its long instinct
for water.

Now she has come. Leading her cows
into the kingdom of cows,
down long winding rivers of cows,
single-file, dust-smoldering processions—
tusked, vigilant, thunder-shaking—
meeting and touching each
to each in the great milling of cows.

Such soft-handed knowing in that fondling
probing lip! Such fingertip-tender
tickling laughter
behind the preposterously old faces—
Even *elephant* is not word enough!

The rivers are jubilant!
The mud holes grow deeper!
She has come,
a black cloud
bringing a black cloud
to a land like her very skin!

Earth shaker! Bellower! Maker of rain!

BELUGA

What were once perhaps arms have simplified in time
to water wings, undulant and white in a black sea
pearled and catacombed with ice.
                                    Pelvis has vanished,
or is at most vestigial, tapering to feet turned tail fin
in a slow fan of somnolent propulsion,
dream-lazy, ghostly.
                       Her call, her only weapon,
is sonar deadly, a stun gun, prelude
to instant swallowing and digestion, death
under anesthetic.
                    The world of stars and sun
and the hard crust of earth
betrayed her, though she visits still,
white in the white moonlight—
                                          the dome of her mind
grown huge and forgiving in the cave of the sea.

BLACK WOLF AT MIDNIGHT

    (after the print by Robert Bateman)

At first we do not see the eyes—
bewitched, bewitching—only trees,

their latticework of iced branches
glittering where moonlight patches

the dark, where any moment centuries
old stone cold silence threatens

to crack like ice the thin bark
in the eternal click, click

of minerals in the soft shift of wind.
Some moccasined tracker in skins

crouched under stars, cold heart
in his mouth, might have stared out

and seen, for the first time,
the colossal foot—hairy, snow-rimed—

planted too eerily close. Dread
paw of the wolf feathering upward

to where the gray column of leg dwarfs
the wrist-thick trunks of the light-starved

trees. Then fathomless bulk
of black body and mystic gold

eyes latched onto him there in that

first dark. Ours is the more distant

wonder of Art, that he could do this
so stealthily, shrewdly, our eyes

tuned to these eyes, our gaze
fixed to this stare without remorse

or malice, a criminal angel's—
our shadow brother lost, ageless

heart of the forest.

AMONG MUSHERS

—in memory of Charlie Belford, DVM

There is something old and beautiful
about the great dog men of the snow,
cussed, crafty as they are
about their tricks of trade.
Trickery is for them serious business
sacred to the dog god as to the wolf god,
confessed, years later, in mock-serious tones—
slow smiles spreading among granite faces.
Young and fierce, they kept the silence
of snow, the blood-oaths of black cold.
Their hands are scarred like fishermen's or farmers'.
They'll trust a good dog before a good man
and a good woman before either.
They share the broke bones and blood sagas
of bull riders. What saved them was a dog
or their wits, or some goddamned good luck.
What you feel, even if you're not one of them,
is flint and fire, laughter out of cold stars.

PILGRIMAGE

      —in memory of Roland Lombard, DVM

I have entered the circle of old men.
They are "talking dogs" and I have been invited.
Outside in the October chill, the dogs are restless.
We hear their chains jingling, sense their feet
quick-dancing, their new fur rippling and attentive.
We know their Asiatic eyes are bright as stars
after first snow—they who come from a world
with 200 words for snow.
                    Inside, the first man speaks.
He has a womanizer's easy smile, a slaver's hard laugh.
He's run with the best and beaten them.
He tells of being chased by wolves, a panicky jab
of a ski-pole into the haunch of a dog
suddenly crouched and frightened—the yelp,
the burst of speed. He tells of later
fastening that ski-pole to the sled frame
just at dog eye-level, banishing forever
the big gray's shrewd laziness.
                    The next
draws slow on a cigarette, speaks slow,
tells of 1400 miles of Antarctic wastes,
crevasses opening like grim mouths, nails
digging in for dear life, the sheer guts,
tirelessness, even the autocratic Byrd's
grudging admiration, despite their small frames.
He smiles then and waits for the third
                        who cannot speak
but has eyes like blue fires, wolf's eyes
under shaggy white brows—patient, fierce,
yet mild in their singleness of purpose.
That he can no longer speak seems proof

he's gone hunting with wolves, entering
their silence like a furred, ghostly god.
He is legend even among the Inuit
for kindness, for indefatigable attention
to detail, able to enter a dog's mind
and bring out the best with no more
than a cluck or gesture—who's felt the wind
of the bull moose charging, the white bear's
shadow, yet come back again and again
to beat the best of the younger men.
It is this quiet the dogs outside are restless for,
his quick signal the hunt is on.
                                        He has fashioned
a model of scapula, humerus and radius/ulna
to show me the shoulder blade's proper rotation.
Outside, he buries my hands in the deep ruff of his leader,
his eyes searching mine for the flicker of comprehension.
Each dog, whirling on its chain like a separate constellation,
keeps eyes riveted on him, waiting for the touch,
the nod, the gesture.
                          A gasp goes up
as we stare into the treacherous ravine that starts
his training trail, now over half a century old.
"He wants to die on the runners," someone whispers.
The first stars have come out, their light perhaps
even colder than wolf's eyes. A hint of snow's
in the air, but also a surge, electric, similar
to a February night I stepped from a Lakota sweat lodge
and stared into buffalo fire—
                                  the horned skull
speaking to the stars.

PHOTOGRAPH: DESERT CANYON

—in memory of Merc Cresap

So time's been here a long time before time
the little nervous ticking
which no doubt brought the photographer
here in the first place on a day like any other
till river time and stone time calmed him
and he saw what? himself in the sun's glow
or the shadow just out of lens range
or his mother's scolding 40 odd years ago
about some distinction of space or order
that rankles him still as he finds the F-stop
to claim the universal light
in the striations of rock
where a river ran through
and truly he is the box canyon of himself
sheared light and shadow
where a river ran through and primordial
wind earth-blood sign and signal
the deep howling of long bad nights for millennia
He'll take it all back to the studio
dancing in his head what might be there
something white hot for cold analysis
the lucent shades of gray
and narrowing edges
editing eventually himself
out of the world forever
yet singing drunken in his darkroom
like God Almighty

VILNIUS GLIMPSES

> *the window is a mirror*
> *where the face merges*
> *with dust and stars*
>   —Kerry Shawn Keys

In the lonely room of the poem

(sifting
plaster dust
and spreading wall
maps of moisture
in the slow
garlic-sour crumble
of old Europe)

the heavy-faced poet ponders the book of losses
dreaming redemption
from the irony and ache of arthritis

or maybe the clatter and clash of sun-bright weapons
as the pagan suicide knights of the forest
vanish into the blood-smoke incense
of the crucifix

but no let up in the relentless walk of the world
eyes dead ahead
ghosts of the mind cops and word killers

and too little mystery or amnesia
in a quart of *degtinė*

no matter the glassy glitter of boutiques
no matter the smart fashion-girls with their cell phones

and small taut buttocks

and the roaring poets of cavernous taverns
blinking into the sun
to mumble poems like apologies
in the still sacred tongue of oak and linden

and placating shrines to the gothic gods of unmaking—
rampant St. George plunging
his lance into the waiting mouth of the monster
and interchangeable saints
wilting like flowers

I want to go home to make love
to my beautiful wife
on the timeless hill of our dreams
stolen from the Iroquois

I want to tear out my teeth in the soundproof
torture chambers of the KGB
and forget the cool-eyed women cut down
in the demystified forest
like a thousand Dianas

I want words to unsay themselves
and the clocks to stop

I want to drink till I drop
and sleep in the gutter
with the rain leaking into my brain
and be bathed in the blood
of inscrutable gutturals
and make a friend of sorrow and terror

I don't want to be written into the heavy book

of the poet with his bitter grief
and Sphinx-like gaze
knowing it all might have been otherwise

though our eyes have met
and there's no going back

READING HEANEY

No need to get carried away the voice
says meaning there'll be time enough for that

life anyway a slow leak back into
stars from that first edge-of-the-world place

bog-rooted and hedged in cow-quivering sleet
and the imperative to keep weather out

along with such novelties and courtesies
and verities of tongue as horse traders use

language come up to look men in the eye
across the pasture gate and slow reticence

of educated hands attaching fact
to fact all the way back to the Bog Man

in his death necklace—
                          though the boy looks out
enthralled by the imperative of dawn

to stop thinking to start it all again—
hear the poem knotted up in the sheep's bleat

or the valley's clattering first hooves of light

DRUM SONG

    —in memory of Ted Hughes

The lightning-flashed hag face of the moor
in the torpor of downpour
and the drizzle-dim skull of Heptenstall

and the curse in the blood of the cursed mud
and Heathcliff's Mother-wound horror
put thistle in the tongue of Yorkshire

the crashing shires and long haul of mountains
where rock and wind ate at each other
and ached for each other like star-crossed lovers

fossilized in poems whose undersong
was the silkiest hands of farmers
coaxing at the womb door

and the galloping gaiety of the otter
slipping his pelt like a sorcerer
and the river's unkillable contradictions and seasons

her unkillable children and thunder

in the big double drum of the heart

Eros/Thanatos   Eros/Thanatos   Eros/Thanatos.

LOWELL

> *In the old New York, we said*
> *"If life could write,*
> *it would have written like us."*

You lost your arid God, His dragon tail
and gorgeous plumage whipping the sea swell
of your Promethean will and thunder
in your "all percussion" obit for the Quaker—
manner or matter your evolving question—
the boy-Keats muscled to the nearly German.

What then? The down look and the letting go,
whiskey glazed eye in false-gold afterglow,
the soft patter of friends no longer pattering,
snippets, smatterings,
crisscrossed conscience and coincidence,
the world's crush
crumpling in a handkerchief—
as if the daze of old age were all day
in a deckchair's decadent complicity
or child's play.

I like the last poems best, their blurry wonder
and disconnects...
the Boston Brahmin with the southern drawl,
vernacular still sparring for the jugular...
the convalescent back from rehab...
seafarer
come home in a New York cab.

TALKIN' BOB'S BLUES

You can't get there from here though you can go a lot of places
In the switchyard of the mind you can rearrange a lot of faces
But the scent of her hair and the touch of her lips and the curse
                                          of her tongue
Say you'll bleed from your eyes till the day you're done

When the plains' red dawns stretch out like lies
And the cut glass of the past gives you spider web eyes
And you feel like you're crawling through the land of the dead
And know the dream of your life should have stayed home in bed

And you don't wanna do what beauty asks
Though she's always there in the mirror's masks
Jean Genet in the role of town crier
Or the vagabond king disguised as vampire

Or the ragamuffin boy who could be anyone
Hank or Woody or the scourge of the sun
Deranging the world to see for the first time
Mississippi was a state of mind
And Desolation just a street sign

You can't get there from here though you jump through hoops
You can dance on the clouds or you can deal from the stoops
Your mama had a sister her sister had a friend
She wanted to bust out he wanted to keep it in
And a baby's cry is the willow's wind
You can't even pray without some kind of sin

Walk down the backstairs slip off in the dark
The devil's face is Joan of Arc's
We might be 40 miles outside of somewhere

But the locals say you can't get there from here

Smoke's been travelin' all through the swamps
Says the trees have been whisperin' the words of *Mein Kampf*
Innocence cries in even the darkest heart
You can die for a rose or you can die for art
And all kinds of things that were wrong from the start

I got a woman behind my door
Says she'll love me but I gotta be poor
Gotta crawl on my knees gotta howl like a dog
But if I'm a prince she'll make me a frog

You can't get there from here though you toss and you turn
And your dreams get heavy and your eyes start to burn
But there's a place you can get to on down the road
Where lying's just another kind of truth in code

And an old man playing a Chinese flute
Says I've had mine you can take the loot
The white beard of nothingness grows from my chin
And the next time we meet we'll all be kin

There's a place I go about a mile from here
Where I take off my face and examine my fear
The lake shines like a mirror and I cup my ear
And nothing much matters but that the words are clear

There are freight cars passing and old crossroads
And dispossessed creeds and broken codes
And dead end dreams where a life implodes
And sometimes you see her dancing in fire
But you can't sing her back from the land of desire

You can bray like a donkey you can caw like a crow

21

There are some kinds of places words can't go
He went down in the valley to sing his song
And let the echo decide if he was right or wrong

He let the echo decide if he was right or wrong

A DREAM OF FALLING

      —in memory of Karl Wallenda

He slept perhaps
the way Sherpas
on a long climb
sleep: on the move,
as though the mountain
were mere dream, and the next step
all that mattered: a hole
pushed into the nothing
that it might vanish
into nothing
and leave him to wake refreshed.

He awoke to a dream
of falling. If there was a scream
it came from another room. It was not
his. He was too transfixed
to scream. He had dreamed the dream
too often.
          But then he had not come
to conquer the mountain. He had done that
years ago: wooed it and brought it to his bed
like a woman. Now he came to the mountain
as a mountain, and dreamed of a man
falling, a man gone suddenly womanish
and expansive, opening his body to sky,
accepting it, as the mountain does, with open arms.

DREAM WALK

THIS, OF COURSE, IS WHAT MONEY WON'T BUY

this hip-to-hip, two-centered circle, drift
and drift—you in front, provocative
as a pomegranate, me in front, hearing
echoes—your footsteps filling mine
the way perhaps snow fills the tracks
of caribou, keeping the wolves off. We're
birds of a feather. Our minds veer
and arc on the same air. It's open season here
on sun and wind, and I'm wearing my license
conspicuous and on my sleeve.

2.

We scuff and boot the leaves like six-year-olds,
grin like raccoons. *These are years*, we say,
*shed like snake skins—doomed, irrelevant,
beautiful.* Miles or years, we've walked
forever here, you and I, putting on
or shedding each other like light or leaves,
the traffic hushed and distant. We feel exotic
as the names of these lakeshore towns we walk in,
the water quiet, leaves falling, the light quixotic.
It's all new. You're new—taut and muscular
as a spring colt claiming his first field.
I'm new—grinning ear to ear, hearing windmills.
Death is new here, too, and moves like water underfoot.

3.

We drift in October light through the rose garden,
all the roses gone. Clothed in purple and black,
you're naked. Naked, raspberries and cream,
you're clothed. It's magic. For you I invent the sun,
feel tragic, drive it to your doorstep
in a long yellow cab, stand there, hat in hand,
like some foolish figure in a thirties' flick—

your hair darker than any back row seat.

4.

You talk, stoop, pick weeds, say *the sky
has breadth. I say birds have scissored
it to death*, but I'm dazzled anyway.
It's late fall. The birds look hungrier.
You say you're leaving your husband anyhow—
for all his good, for all my bad.
Standing against a tree, your hood up,
your half-moon smile floating somewhere
below the hairline, I imagine you grew there
whole, yesterday perhaps, dew-like, and I
kiss you, feel shy, boyish—hungry
the way the old birds must
who don't head south.

5.

It's mid-winter and the crunching underfoot
sounds rare, precious. You're
purple and yellow. I'm fatigue L.L. Bean
gray-green. The six years between us though
is hardly May and January,
and I'm dazzled by purple and yellow
and can outrun you anyway.
You admit now, though, cold hurts,
for all your tough talk. I should admit
what...for all my tough talk?—that my wife
writes, calls, cries, argues, accuses? Indeed
this crunching underfoot is precious—glass
or ice. It's January. It will soon
be May. Our rooms are white and beautiful
and breathe with plants.

6.

Your mother calls, sends chocolates, prays—
makes me feel like the anti-Christ. And
it's true enough I come from a land
of sand and stone, and never put much trust
in trees or green. (In my mind's eye
I always return
to the same rock ridge, almost abstract now
in the blind revision of its lie—
a dark saw-blade raised against blue sky.)
But here, your walk is so much like the sun
or prayer, I must stoop
and touch the place you've stepped, knowing
come spring, something will grow there.

7.

Today bright sun makes blue sky and white birds
pure blue, pure white, barely visible
as we squint and almost stumble
in the pure light.
                      Yet we feel entitled here
as tourists, say, who've paid their fare,
though never dreaming it would look like this.
Beguiled by the low cant of foreign tongues,
we're half afraid some blunt truth in our own talk
will startle us back to earth, bring the dream
crashing like glass about our ears.
                                  But this
is mid-March,
              when the wind blows and the domed sky
holds,
        when small nests of clustered stones
nosing into wind on the iced canal
rise and become birds.
                      This is the season
of the long white distance,
                      when seeing
is much like blindness, blindness like pure sight.

8.

You say, *You are the magician, I but the source.*
Who could top that? Who, mid-stride,
could help but feel the joy
of fear stutter his heart
like cloud-shadow. We have walked
a long time. It is growing dark. I wish
to take you in my arms. I wish to say
to the child we will one day make,
You grew here, among sun and wind
in the gathering dark. I wish to say,
Your mother was taken
for goddess
among stones, among these circling
and calling birds,
                      and they were not far wrong.

9.

We have, I think, no word for this thin-aired
quiet full of light, through which we drift
like new ghosts
wakened to Elysian Fields—the still, green lakes
somnolent as deep thought. It's the day
before Easter. The fishermen
standing on the firm bank
wave their fly-rods like bright wands
toward dark depths
where once new life must have climbed, sloth-like
into a dream of sunlight,
and where now loud children and willing dogs
are all smiles, wagging tongues,
sinew and muscle.
Today we talk less, think more.
Today we smile at all that is sensuous
and literal.

TREES

Today they've come back from the snow—
their dream-walk that began in December—
and are settling in along the ravine
where the creek runs, shaking the fatigue
from their bones, talking softly among themselves.
In a week the elders will speak in tongues.
In two they'll be chanting.
Muskrat will hum.
In a month the blue flower of the lake
will break from her icy spell.

MARCH INVITATION

Today every tree
a hand of withheld fire
twisted and passionate against the sky—

Rain back to snow, indecisive,
gusts into a sleety, crow-battering wind
combing lusterless scraggy hills,

sifting the sick fields—loam-scent
rising like a witch-brew elixir
from the crushed pterodactyl skull
of last year's robin.

O ravenous mouth making trees shiver,
the black hearts shudder—

If they knew the glad-hand light of summer
working them like a politician full of promises,
how could they forget in their slag-sleep
this whispery touch, this tingling wakefulness
under the dark dreaming magma of sky?

But their amnesia grows perfect again—
O schoolgirls in the hands of the March wind!

THE MOUNTAIN

The mountain
at the south gateway
of our glacier lake (still white as satin
in late March) is more glorified hill
than mountain,
                but with the sullen blue presence
of mountain, a sort of brow ridge
thrust up from the softer brown thighs
of the other hills—
                bouldered in Pleistocene sleep,
a hill, like Cézanne's, a man
could walk around for years
and get lost in, his eye cutting
narrow goat paths of perfect
clarity.   So hill becomes mountain
in a vibration of eye waves, in the forgetting
of tedious plains thrust up out of
sea bottom shiftlessness—
                      leans hard
in the wind, poised toward some moment
it has lost all track of.

GEESE

Over hills russetted by the late sun
and the silent underfires of hard winter
the geese rise—

They rise over yesterday's white lake,
today a sudden fiery blue,
into coppery, blood-thirsty, perfect sky.

Suddenly I understand their struggle with sun—
it is a wound, their wound. They are bathed in blood
as they rise, necks craned, shuffling, regrouping,

finding their bearings, gathering the sun's power
into their left eye and along their immaculate, outstretched
identical bodies, while below them

the jesterings of black birds in twos and threes
ape their gigantic herding, tittering
at the titanic effortings, swooping and plunging

but wishing them well—or not well
but farewell. While I, chilled and breathless,
take my own chance in the last light

and dance with the oldest tree
on my property, a twisted old apple, all elbows
and shudderings, beaks and talons, a crone

of unparalleled eloquence and elongations,
simperings and croonings, a cackling
of refracted lights and reddening shawls,

burnt siennas, rising as the geese rise
and dancing to the goose's song
until the geese are gone.

FOG

We woke
to cathedrals
of fog—spires, robes, angels—
valhallas of choral voiced silence.
Its breath obliterated farms,
rode the lake's abyss like a warship.
It took the antlers of trees as its standards.
It marched north along roads
whose cars blundered over ridges
like sleepy cattle. Crocuses
brightened like tiny suns
in the sulfurous galaxies of mosses.
On the second day, it lost pomp and contour.
Drum-silent, it lay moiling over hills in listless aftermath.
It clung to our eye-corners like sooty laundry.
By the third day, the tittering of birds was strange.
Their calls vibrated through invisible holes in our bodies.
Our mouths hung stupidly open—our eyes
merely the shifting mirrors of fog. Our hearing
crept out over fields without hope or longing.

NIGHTWOOD

The dogs tell me they've come—
a skin crawling, fur bristling,
alert, faces-in-the-moonlight
statuary stillness, pressuring
a slight yelp from the youngest.

Something come down in the midnight
from behind the hill's eyelid
travels with the patience of the blind—
browses and peers in at us
with unearthly eyes, as though

the lights of our house were hellfire
guarded by wolves, a terror
that lures them out of slow-chewing
sidelong glances, flickering
uncertainty, sudden hoof-thump

oaken vigilance—something more near
than heartbeat, but older, antlered,
waist-deep in the sky-deep blackness—
ghosts older than the Iroquois
turned back into trees by the dawn.

HAWK

Dark-rumored inkling of air-chills,
pulsing pupils, the whole hill
monastery-still, a tilting
cliff's edge empty
reckoning—blue water, blue sky.

Ponderous, as if in chains,
attended by black birds, he rises
out of the tree-fringe
hoisted by huge shoulders, granite facemask
blank as an angel's

over the flapping canopy of lake
unwavering and undeterred, past lake rim and horizon
into miraculous high noon
where he who owns nothing, not shadow or hunger
absolves utterly,

becomes nothing—all shadow, all hunger—
the eye-scorching sun unmasked in its bottomless plummet.

SOLSTICE

This afternoon green, angel-winged, shimmering
summer is upon us, a solemn shadowed, silky
sibilant rejoicing of gnats and dragonflies
in heart-throb stillness.

Only the purr of her engines, in full throttle,
disrupts the fish-silence of stars, the Scheherezade
dawn-silvering, moon-mingling, dusk-moiling
blossom of the lake, my son's face

rapt in the reflected bauble of the world.
We fall down like the stars and we die
mutters the machinery of the green woods,
inventing the full weight of the sun,

its canopied light, wing-pulse murmurings.
We rain down like the sun
                              and he smiles, he smiles.

RACOON

Days past death, he was decomposing
in a ditch by the roadside,
body gossamered by maggots,
haloed by shed, fine fur,
the black swoon of his limbs
grease for the black oil of earth,
his head no longer head
but the mask of an angel's
upward gaze, the shrunk hands
supplicant.
         Into the murderous
innocence of night, he'd come
strolling, with hands of a jewel thief,
eyes of a gypsy—knocked dead
in a moment.
            The dawn did not mourn him
but lit up the last silvering of his pelt.
The crows pecked at him and savored his eyes.
The maggots swarmed him.
All that pilfering would end soon.
By morning, the curved struts of his keel bone
would house only wind crossing
the leeching black ooze of his emptiness.

NIGHTSCAPE

The lake tonight is river in the sultry South,
still, smoky, under insect chirr
and black, swampy boughs. A single dock light
claims its lance of silver water
that means loneliness, or hope, or beauty's
steely, soft indifference to beauty.
Out there the old river is speaking to no one
and no one is listening. The half moon
rising is pure Islam. Even my bones know
wherever they are is home.

DIFFUSIONS OF AUGUST

Somewhere, I think, there lurks a poem today—
aching perhaps on the horizon
or in the lost last blue sky of summer.

"I stay indoors and spoil another season"
wrote the old master,
searching the moment within a moment

when the present fades
and there is only the present—
to walk forth crippled thereafter.

Bless us with this curse lisp the thick leaves
with their fat shadows, sibyls
of midnight, silvery wombs of the morning.

The spidery breeze on my face
has come its thousand miles.
The tall trees honor me.

I walk among mountains
and know the angels' names.
I drag my lame foot and feel the beggar's shame.

"They want me to wear old clothes…
not walk in the painted sunshine…
but live in the tragic world."

Hail to thee, dark talkers,
shakers of leaves,
whispering still in the soft air,

in the lazy air,
as insects rattled in the golden blaze
when the poem got made.

AT TWILIGHT

Fatherless among the animals I wake in the half-light
sinless as a June bug pure as Narcissus
I am what I look at
The leaves see me and know my smell
What I touch touches me back
I cannot know whether I am the flower
or the flower of the flower
or just smooth water
reflecting tree more ravishing than tree
flower more wayward than flower

when your witch-light comes like gossamer
brushing my cheek

SOMETIME BEFORE WORDS PERHAPS

your arm moved—
a glitter of small hinges.
Or was it your leg,
its calculated unwinding?

I was asleep, say,
or lost in thought.
I heard your blood
though, how it sang,

and I felt your cloud shadow
coming, crossing my face.
I looked—
you were full of yourself

dancing. I looked—
you were the waterfall of yourself
dancing. I looked—
your breath drank my eyes.

I listened—your feet drummed
shut my ears. I groped,
but your skin turned fingers
to spider webs.
              Sometime,
out of the dark of my body,
I spoke.

HER DALLIANCE

Between her fingers
the plucked stalk of your brainstem
blossoms

petal by petal in the empty air.
Between her toes
Tigris and Euphrates divide

and multiply. She loves you.
She loves you not.
Perhaps you are the pinprick rain

on the sheer face of an autumn lake.
Perhaps you are snow.
She is dreaming of crossroads

and you are the emptiness.
She is playing with dolls
and you are the mad muttering.

She is gossiping by the well
and you are the strewn fieldstones,
lidless eyes of the desert

waiting for rain. Her indecision
is delicious with cunning.
The mountains heave. Your leaves shiver.

TIGER DANCE

She is the languid, languorous
disease of the sun, flower
of his passion, hint
of his corruption among shadows.

He comes to her disguised
as her double, only larger,
more impossibly brutal-beautiful—
his face a Paleolithic sun shower.

She in turn turns tiger lily,
all smiles and pussycat frailty
shivery under his touch—
needier, whorier

than his lewdest imaginings—
his great winking anus
laughing at the winking
gay forest above them.

This is he who has hugged
and scarred the trees
as his vassals, whose gape
at her nape is the very vault of heaven.

This is she
who releases him,
brings on the darkness,
leaves him free again to love nothing.

TODAY PERHAPS THE LIZARD

who lies down in his own shadow
inventing the sun through half-closed eyes,
feels his skin, thickening with years,
grow nervous as water.
Perhaps he just feels lucky.

You keep coming back like a dream.
Your hips make light shiver,
make me peer up silly-sideways
like an old dog
to watch the bonfire of your bones.

Night's coming, though.
The sky blue water
of your eyes will turn dark
then. Stars will come out.

Tomorrow
you will come and go again
like a river—
              your bright bones
stealing my shadow.

ALWAYS

under the leaves there was death waiting,
despite your tuned, high-voltage body.

Tigers and rivers glide in us nameless
but the day fades and it is never enough.

The poem deconstructing was an old saw
but we made honey in its warm cauldron

and I said *love* with the white mouth
of the moonflower, with iridescent suns

of coneflowers flaunting whispery black eyes.
It was summer in the garden where you moved

without burden of self like a cloud, paused,
looked, shifting your glorious haunches

like any happy horse claiming its field—
all heat and hunger and applause.

SCOFFERS

This morning a wide-fingered hand
crossed the hood of my car
like a great ray—undulant, ghostly,
more mind-shadow across adobe wall
than simple crow wing's sudden dark
against the metal sheen.
                      Later,
shadowy among trees, their calling
unnerved me, creaking like oarlocks,
and their flapping, eavesdropping absences
pestered my eye-corners—laughter
like bitten off blood-oaths
flung loveless to summer skies, undermining
even the jeweled lichens, the great cascading
cliffs of leaves.
                  And now in a boggy valley
atop the mast-high skeletons of elms,
they cluster like thieves on yardarms
or the tattered crest-plumes of buried horsemen
come back over deathless snows
to claim the purple of loosestrife,
psalming greens of the rushes—
the pinwheel turnings of death's rainbow
in each small, malevolent eye.

OCTOBER SUN

Weeks since the sun came. Now its crescendo
dazzles the landscape in a thunder of wind
and flaming holy trees. By four, it's gone—
from gilded hills, wide-skirted valleys.
And we, changed, like boatmen come back
over the sliding gray river of clouds
having looked into fire—we've danced
tipsy under the red-eyed sun. Nothing
so deadly as winter can happen now,
we have sun's promise.
                              And the leaves?
They too have a promise—to vessel
the whirl of his fire
into the whorl of the earth
with no more than a thin mad whisper to go on.

GHOST MOON

haunted by cries on a November afternoon.
The geese, with their compass needle necks,
their tumultuous hurry

are passing, have been passing
for days. Each with a piece of magnetic field
planted deep behind its sun-fired eye

heading south. Jostled by wind, pelted
by rain. *Unlikely, unlikely*
their cacophonous holler, their harpy wail.

Something of us goes with them,
feels the ebb in the blood tides
and salt marshes, the emptiness, the cold.

THE ROAD HOME, NOVEMBER

Twilight needling the eye—the fogged out,
whited out road collapsing
into goblin namelessness, withering
weird trees, half-light lure
of dog and deer
in the treacherous bearded fields—

Giving in to centuries-old, no-world silence—
head down, nape-of-the-neck
bristling attention
to far star-cauldron nothingness—

Papery-skulled, haggard
from the hard voiced night,
I come to myself
building a fire—webby, ochre light,
oily shadows, elemental
Stonehenge geometry of logs, inscrutable
as the star-crossed bones of bison
bruise-blotting the clammy walls of the caves.

Later my son's raw edged ancient crying
and soft-haired nuzzling.

THE LANDSCAPE OF MISSING YOU

Something beautiful at the bottom of somewhere eludes me
The lake is too white and cold to love
Our hopped-up neighbors ephemeral as fog
My life is an absence among scraggly hills
and the valley's bottom-feeders
Too cold for humanity
No honor among thieves
The wind blows
The trees endure
Whatever the ache at the bottom of winter
only you afloat over Asia
comfort me—
only the angels of your approaching thighs

I am tired of my country of robots and outlaws
The best of myself is smaller than a thimble
Bring me the sun O my wanton one

A MOMENT IN FEBRUARY

It is the light at the center of every cell.
      —Mary Oliver

See how the silky sun floods the ermine fields—
ton on ton of sheer white light
tumbling kid-gloved soft—each sun-swooned tree
transfixed, snow-mittened, bowed as in prayer.
These are the plains of Xanadu
tilting skyward, the high steppes of the Horseman.
Or this is upstate New York shaken
by the vast pastness of the heart, journeys leading nowhere
but here—sun on the snow, the slurred fur
of feel. And everywhere, tremulous,
a shout!

ONCE

    (with some thefts from Simin Behbehani)

I came to you as if from a far country
The night was not quite in your eyes
but the evening smoke and the roses of your skin
met in purple shadows

I came through the vague veiled streets
toward some clarity or hunger
You were my fire in the moth-light
my confessor

You danced the stars blind under the witching moon
I crawled in your darkness like the tapping beetle
Our mouths met

Dawn in the desert is a million gold butterflies—
I lived there once among broken stones
husks of bodies
a tale of death and deaths
and women turned to salt
under stubborn hummocks of black cloth

We grow old like the cracking clay
of forgotten rivers
Soon no one will remember our voices
or the glancing light of our tremulous
tremors

Was it the wind I came on
lipping your waters
combing the sunlight scarves across your throat

So often now we are tired
and old women I once knew laugh softly
behind the curtain
and the mud of the riverbank
squelches under their feet

I came through bulrushes over moon-glazed bayous
and our bodies became snake-dancing
cranes
feathery cries

We cannot love each other forever
except as the stars do
all flame and nothingness

Our skins will grow worn and frail
as papyrus leaves
locust wings
May the burden of pain bring lightness

We lie down to take flight
like the desert sand under the scour of wind

I came like a sea eagle out of the sun's eye
to whirl you talon in talon
down the roller coaster sky

I met your gaze in the forest of being

The rest was just history

A DANCE OF STONE

For beauty's nothing but the beginning of terror

Rilke

For my brother Stephen

UR OF THE CHALDEES, 1958

They are like aliens on the moon, the Americans—
bermuda shorts and cameras, pudgy, pale,
a little queasy from the train ride.
Dust from the storm in the night
has permeated everything they own
down to the skin.
They are not quite certain why they came,
and wear the baffled, blinking looks of baby birds.

The hole in the ground is the biggest I've ever seen,
with "evidence of the flood"—a four foot wide ribbon
of sand half way up the sides of an otherwise brown pit
strewn with broken bits of pottery. Local kids, urchins,
scamper down the steep, thin path at break-neck speed
for *rials* and *dinars*. They seem to have sprung up here
without benefit of parents or care. Across
the millennia, I feel the closeness of children
and the terrible price of money.

After a long climb, I am first to reach the summit
of the ziggurat
and so enter the dusky sky of Abraham.
I am 10. My heart is a drum.
I stand at the top of the god-forsaken world.

COW SKULL

This is the land's death mask—the splintered face
into which earth's bodiless distances
bulldozed to a halt—
                       the great brain
ousted by wasp nest, sagebrush thrust
from the caved nostrils.
                       You would think
staring into the round gaping eye
that nothing could have died so utterly.

On the horizon, the stone town darkens
and turns blue. Soon it too
will fall to ruin—
                       like the honed cheek
of the cow's skull, turn to a husk
in the evening air—
                       while dry, bird-like men
come picking their way homeward
over the broken fields.

THE EGG WOMAN

She has no teeth, and if she cries at all
it is not with her eyes, for they have gone
beyond the dark reaches of her face
long ago.
    Her attitude is utter blindness
though she sees perfectly well, crossing our ridge,
eggs cradled in her stolen paint cans, bent back
dropping behind a boulder, as if feeling her way
far back, down some dark place in the landscape
only she knows.
    And as the locals tell it
(and they are fond of telling it) before the fire,
before the catastrophe that brought down
home, poverty, old age, all in a single
combustible moment,
       she was far the richest whore
in all Khuzistan, with silks and tapestries to boot.

But these are rumors. These hills are filled
with rumors, the muttering of cripples,
the crying of children.

HANOON

Our cook, Hanoon, tells me he is a Chaldean,
displaced by who knows how many migrations,
murders, to come to live in Braim Village
along the river green with date palms,
cool in its dark mud huts even in summer,
though he must ride to our house across
the blazing salt flats on a comic huge bicycle
wearing a pith helmet. His teeth are oddly dark
along the gums, though serving as wire cutters
when he needs them.
                        He wrings the neck of a chicken
and we laugh to see it scuttle in crazed circles
crashing into the walls of the compound. So death
is right here with us always, and maybe
we too are crazy chickens.
                        When I am eleven,
we come to dine at his village. He is something
like a Head Man, and we are given fesenjahn
that looks like mud and tastes like ambrosia.
We eat from a common bowl with our hands,
and for the first time I feel holy.
                        In the bazaar,
the beggar boys scatter like startled birds
at a single hissing whisper from his lips,
his hands fluttering like quick black bats.
                        For hours
he squats at cards, slapping them down with true
gambler's relish – his big, bare, broad feet,
so quiet as he pads, cat-like, about the house,
planted happily on the wide earth,
his pock-marked face smiling
like a black leopard's.
                        Years later,

we'll lure him with money to another town
far from his family and tribe,
to live, displaced, among the grim Baktiari.
And he will service us, less smiling than before,
and steal our silver, and we will fire him,
and I will know what it is like
to steal a man's joy and pride
and break his heart.

In my dreams, I break bread with him still.

ALONG THE AVENUE OF DEAD GESTURES

Surely there have been darknesses
before this one,
              growing between the doors,
moving as I move
                    down the cobbled streets
full of the vacant eyes, thick thighs and gold teeth
of the women who work them.
                              Bones rotted before these,
or the round skull of the child froze
in the broad, bloodless face
of the whore.
              After me, there will come other deaths.
Others will walk home by the back roads

IN THE BAZAAR, THE LAYING ON OF HANDS

              As in the lightning-bolt
suddenness of mountain, the road below
abruptly liquid and lashing—a face
come up out of sea of faces, sharper,
larger, like a great boulder, opening
in the oppressive heat—
                               not a cry
so much as a lifted up blackness
out of the belly's pit, a momentary
moronic braying ravaged forever
by the drum-roll haggling of hawkers,
vendors, the donkeys' needle-like hooves
sharpening under the massive heave of their burdens.

THE WIND-CURVED SANDHILLS

> *And make mention of the brother of Aad when he warned his folk of among the wind-curved sandhills—and verily warners came and went before and after him—saying: serve none but Allah. Lo! I fear for you the doom of tremendous day.*
> —the Koran

First there comes the large rasping voice
among the dunes, and the men moving toward it—
sun baked, humorless men, who stand or squat,
occasionally muttering among themselves.
Today they learn about the pain of generation,
the thanklessness of youth: how a woman
nurtures a man for forty years
and gains nothing: learn, too,
how a dark storm cloud will dissolve
into the thunder of hooves; and how,
after that, villages will stand empty
but for the wind.
                    At noon, food is brought out
on large platters, the water in goatskins.

★ ★ ★

Later, toward evening, a man squats in his tent
speaking as though into his hands. He wants,
somehow, to reach this gaunt, patient woman
who squats and rocks on her heels, nursing a child.

She remains skeptical, incurious—
her dark eyes distant, her face hard.

Suddenly he stops speaking and begins

gouging absurd little stick figures
in the dirt. He has the words wrong he explains.
He will go listen again tomorrow.

She nods and smiles and goes on suckling the child.
He stares back sheepishly into his hands.
Looking at him now, she may almost imagine
how, in a few years time, this shy, brooding face
will burst through doors,
       and how the children
crouching inside will scream.

★   ★   ★

         It is twilight
and a man moves quietly among the dunes.
Reaching a ridge
     he kneels down in deep sand.
He thinks he hears a voice.
       What he hears
is the wind gnawing the tough tendrils of grass
at the dune's lip.
     Taking a handful of sand
he begins pouring it over his head.
He pours another
     and another.
        He thinks
the sand is water,
   or tears,
     or perhaps even stars.

A DANCE OF STONE

> *Whoso ascribeth partners unto Allah hath wandered far astray.*
> *They invoke in his stead only females; they pray to none else*
> *Than Satan, a rebel... As for those women who are found guilty*
> *Of lewdness... confine them to their houses until death take*
> *them.*
>   —the Koran

For six long days they have surrounded my house—
these fat, squat men crouching upon their hams,
having their food brought out to them – eating,
leering, and licking their thick fingers. Six
long days. And on the seventh, I shall die.

I can remember how my father knelt
for hours before the stone goddess, a hard man.
And when he took me in his arms and squeezed,
I wished, sometimes, I too were stone. At night
he loved my mother hard. From where I lay,
I'd see her face grow larger and more craven
until, at least, she'd scream. Her face grew calm
then, calm and small, like that of the stone goddess.

The night of the long scream, when the men came
with large, torch-lit faces and killed my father,
I didn't cry. My mother screamed and her face
grew large. And he was small then, small and broken
like the stone goddess. But I didn't cry.

And then the men with torches and large faces
took me with them, and, for a time, were kind.
They told me of a strong god who was kind
to women, merciful they said, because
women were weak. And as I grew older,

they came to me at night and brought me gifts
and told me how my breasts grew large. At dawn
they cursed me, saying it was they who were weak.

I grew distrustful then, though never showed it.
I took their gifts: this house, the serving
man they gave me. Agreed, also, to consort
no more with the good women of their tribe,
but only with this single serving man.

And still at night they came to me with gifts,
but spoke no more about their strong, kind god.
Once, in the night, one brought my father's goddess—
charred, broken—saying how I might mend her.
I cried then, cried for having once forgotten
how small she was, and broken, and but half
understood—cried in words I hardly understood.
And the years passed. And still at dawn they cursed me.

At last, this six days past, the elders came
and cursed me then in earnest, said my house
was Satan's house and my gods Satan's gods.
They took my goods, my food, the serving man
they'd given. When they left, they locked the door.

I screamed then, tearing at my clothes, my hair.
I clawed great furrows in my face and breasts.
And feeling how my own blood ran, I cursed them—
cursed just to see them there, squatting and leering,
having their food brought out to them. At first
I cursed only in their own blunt, thick tongue.
Later, in the smooth language of my father.

At this they laughed and jeered and threw small stones.
I saw their hatred then, their fear, and I screamed

louder and longer, cursed until I fell
exhausted. Then they laughed again and asked
what good my father's stone could do me now.

Becoming calm, I went deep into my house,
far from the shouting and the stones. They fear
this silence, I said, fear my stillness. From me
they want only some mad, lewd dance, not quiet—
they do not want me dead, only to die.
And I took up my goddess, spoke to her
and made her whole, finding what I had half
known, half forgotten—the stone goddess dances.

Tomorrow when they enter into my house,
they shall come quietly, afraid, as if
into a shrine. And I shall dance for them—
dance of my father and my father's people—
a strong dance, a good dance, a dance of stone.

HEAT

Day without plot. Fixtured and fissured. Fractured beyond measure.

I have known heat to stretch horizon to horizon
Like bright steel—a metal or mica or star-scattered heaven
Foundering the mind. Thick-tongued and wordless. White sand
On black brain. Blood rivered in suet. A pocket
Picked empty as wind.
                        Nothing moves in such heat,
Not lizard or scorpion, sandfly or shadow. Tree
Becomes rock, becomes gray husk, becomes
Ruinous. Squalor of sand. Numbness of sun.
                                      To squat there,
The stones of your absence in your hands,
Is to squat in the center of silence forever.
It is to hold the sun like water in the crumbling of your hands.

It is to hold the bright day. Sun. Sand. A dun-colored dog

Disappearing into a distance of sun and sand—
Humped, slavering. The steady
Rise and fall of the four flickering paws
Too maniacally silent and concentrated for even
The loose gesture of wind to intrude on.
                                        Or the dream of day,
A child's sorrowing and dreaming—aftermath
Of that too much excitement. Four boys with baseball bats
Who had braved what they knew of the horrors
Of the desert, a compound of mad dogs
And oil drums,
            barbed wire and heat,
A dun-colored dog disappearing into desert like a dead wind.

It hangs like a daydream of fish in the sun's eye. Fish flying

Like birds above the thunder of dynamite, burble of river,
Then falling to flotsam. Fish by the armload,
Blind, dazed, flaccid as faith. A stench
Ripping open the whole length of the gullet of sky
And left for foxes and flies.
      A day I walked in sun
Unstable as the dynamite I carried in a brown paper sack
Like in indigestible lunch.
       And threw. And walked. And threw.
And watched the shards of hillside rise
Like torn brains to hang in the hair of scrub-trees
While the lizard sang silent in the sun—the blood-
Throated lizard, bloated and bragging in the swaggering sun.

Or the daydream of glass. White light. Bone light. The sailing
of glass—

Shards of pottery heaped in domes
Where ziggurats grew round in wind
And the tombs of kings
Stunk with centuries of fox.
　　　　　　　　　　The sun was a blind mad eye
Carved on an obsidian stairway to heaven
Where the fallen bulls of stone
Offered their great backs to me to ride
And dust filled the air like glass.
　　　　　　　　　　　Mother's eyes were black fires
As she hurled ashtrays and plates, bowls and crystal
At walls and mirrors. Her voice
Was glass breaking. Her breath was ether.
　　　　　　　　　　　　　　The stench of fox,
Like the burning of flesh, stayed in my nostrils for days.

A dream before I knew you, met you. Though I knew of your
                                                      absence.

I knew of Lydia Cathcart who spread her great thighs
On the Riding Club couch or across
The great outcropped boulders of the desert
For grooms and stable hands.
                           I knew of her husband's
Straw-colored pomaded hair and creased
High-fashion trousers,
                     and how her eyes bugged out a little
And spittle formed at the edges of her mouth.
                                    Akbar,
Who would die in the advanced stages of syphilis,
Served out drinks and food, laughed
Like a girl, and kissed me when he could.
I knew of your absence. And I dreamed of Lydia Cathcart.

And of women on horseback—long shadows in the deep hills.

And one who rode a stallion like a black wind
That even I could not ride,
                              her hair a raven black.
And then the horse who fell and bled for me,
A deep pocket of blood forming between his forelegs
Like a breast—
                a black horse with a girl's mane
And a king's name.
                      And then the dream of women
Ridden by men or boys
In the twilit paddock, moving
Down the long hill in the long heat, arm
In arm, indifferent to all but the long loneliness
Of the first stars rising,
                        the glittering of raw, fierce weapons.

And the desert rises then in the twilight. It lifts

Its burnt body out of itself. The scabs of its flesh
Soften. It sings in its silence like an old woman
And becomes young again.
                          Her sands glitter in moonlight.
Her ridges rise like deep rivers entering the sea of stars.
Her foxes find new stealth,
                    their fur bristles.
Snakes slither from dark dens with eyes like stars
And tongues like the singing of stars.
                                This is the clarity
Of fire.
        This is the clarity of the long bones of the hills
Rubbing together like the thighs of the long woman
Buried among them.
                This is death.
This is the white-hot crotch of death, blue as a diamond.

>   And Gafoor smokes his hookah with yellow eyes. Rocks
>
> And claps his thighs. Dreams himself. Stinks of horse,
> Stinks of women, stinks of the sun and the sun's lies,
> The long ride.
>   And the round stones of the moonlight
> Are the hunched backs of the night's feeders
> Who rise and walk—
>   Or the arched bellies of the night's
> Eaten. Who do not get up. Who turn on themselves
> Like sculpture. Blue stones.
>   And the tarantula
> Rising like smoke
>   sings to his green-eyed mate
> Under the arched light of her dark sting,
> And dances there in the round light.
>   Long night.
> The yellow-eyed. Soft-thighed. Torn and turning.

And then shard-light in the broken east and the stones' cry—

The huddled bones,
Carcass and carcass. Confession of sand,
Celebration of wind.
                       And bright blood blooms in the desert
As the blind white fish
Flounder from withered pond
To withered pond
Where once the river flowed hard
In the moonlight.
                Achilles died
That Odysseus might live—the heartless heart
Succumbing to the body's stealth,
                              the moon-fired fox,
Skulking and singing, meeting the dawn's dead eye.

O daughter of days. Mother of nights. If I have sought women

As the sun
Seeks water,
        eye
In eye,
    tear
        and muscle,
                forgive me the long chains'
Shackle and shackle. Forgive me the great bull-bones
Of the world in the sun,
        and hold me now in the implacable
Pallor of your gaze, this improbable poise
Of full moon at dawn's edge—
        Bone-song,
                wind-haunt,
Voice of the fathers
And the father of voice—
        Bring back
The great wind,
    sing me the singing,
        the great song—

O blood of the mothers who labored long!

INNER SANCTUM

Anood and Matrood Jassemzahdi
have long since moved from their home by the courts
to the low mud huts of Braim Village.
Years have passed since our tennis days
and I am crossing the barren flats for the last time,
feeling the heat rise through the soles of my shoes,
seeing it waver, silvery-blue, as the black-green
date palms near the river grow
imperceptibly closer.
                    The heat is an odd familiar.
It holds me in its palm like a puppet.
The dizzying distance of the flats to the north
could be glare ice, polar smoke, or the timeless lake
it once was.
             Miles and miles and miles
the mind sails as the feet plod
a few hundred yards. Sunstroke, heatstroke,
are states of mind almost religious, the body
spooling off into darkness.
                  The narrow
dark paths of the village are welcoming
labyrinthine passageways, silvery-blue
eyes of trachoma flickering in the shadows.
My hands grope for a few cool coins
to assuage the heat of conscience.
                        The doorway
is there—a few low-ceilinged rooms
fanning off from the courtyard, palatial
by village standards—the swept dirt floors,
open spigot in the courtyard,
and the *chador*-draped figures of Mother
and Sister, two silent hearth goddesses

of the cave-cool gloom, mourners of a life
more ancient than I can imagine.
                              In just such a room
Christ, the wanderer, must have had his weary feet bathed,
with just such sure strong hands as theirs.
                                        And for his crown
he must have worn just such camel-thorns
as I have idly scuffed in coming—
                              anything like a rose
rare in these parts.

OLD MOUNTAINS

There were mountains in the old place,
the place of old bones, and the mountains
were like bones, only browner, sandstone,
though sometimes bleached pale as bones.
And dark goats moved among them,
and the people who grew out of them
were like goats, small and dark
and quick when the sun was not pure
poison, moving about their business
which was not our business, theirs
being soil, which there wasn't much of,
ours being oil, which came out of the ground
by the ton and snaked through the hills
and desert in pipelines inevitable
as the azure, steel sky itself. Perhaps
they were not real mountains so much
as up-thrust foothills, craggy plateau
a man or goat could climb in a day,
stand at the top of, and feel Moses
come down from.   They were holy mountains,
and under the holy mountains was oil
that sometimes still made bushes burn
or the Red Sea part for the islands
of deep-bellied freighters, pregnant
with crude.   And if they were not mountains,
they were at least the high steppes
of the horsemen, grown ghostly with time,
and my sleeper's body slept among them,
and my dreamer's body, which was only smoke
from village chimneys in winter, or the black

eyes of the skulls of their huts in summer,
saw the quick shimmering emerald of the fields
and crevices in spring, the flash of the bright-dressed
girls of the waterhole, their ankle bracelets
saucy as the glitter of crime in Salome's eyes,
and the black eyes under the black wind
of the black *chadora*
billowing around the husks of crones.
They were the sacred mountains camped
at our outskirts, while our fathers
mined oil from beneath them and hardly
saw them.
          But their graves sang to us
in the evenings, and the thin smoke
of their cook-fires rose like ghosts,
and they lay down with us in our dreams
like beasts, breathing and patient.
                              "Ours,"
we thought, as the Persian blue sky
swaddled their shoulders, as the black
night sky lay down on their backs
with its pinprick stars. They rose
like continents in the black sea
of nightfall, then rose again like the skulls
of sacrificial beasts in the dawn. And perhaps
our white mothers heard them and started
drinking harder, savaging the servants,
quarreling with our sad sack fathers.
Distracted in the midnight, they paced cold tiles,
their bare feet lisping the hours—
ethereal, haughty, silken whisperings.
And the mountains were theirs, too,
and the dirty hands of the servants
who needed such scolding. Some absence
lurked in their eyes like the shadows

of mountains, among the coffee klatches
and beer-swilling mornings.
                            But we
were the children of the mountains,
and they entered us as easily as sky,
as easily as night, and what they showed us
was fire and shadow, dancers under the worn moon.
And we saw how time moved in ripples toward the horizon,
shuddering under the noonday sun. They moved
in us like the spirits of Alexander or Herod,
Nebuchadnezzar, Ashurbanipal, Xerxes
or Ataxerxes—slow fires
in the waking midnight.
                        And our incongruous
fathers waited at the bus stop – white,
short-sleeved shirts, clip-on ties
and crew cuts. They talked of Oklahoma
or L.A., Atlantic City or Baton Rouge,
but never of the bleached mountains
on the hem of whose skirts they stood
dazed in the morning light. Their gaze
was too calculated, the sheaves of paper
in their briefcases too diagrammatic
and impersonal. Children of the Depression,
their souls had suffered foreclosure.
They had bankers' eyes.
                        They are mostly
dead now, copies of *Forbes Magazine*
strewn on the night table. And we
who were children of the mountains
search nightly on the News for glimpses
of the pale, pitiless sleepers—there
behind the reporter with blank banker's eyes,
beyond the rolling dust of tanks, bomb blasts
and squalor, the rubble of apocalypse.

We have joined the absent ones.
Nothing there now remembers us but the mountains
etched behind our eyelids.

LAMENTATIONS

ALEXANDRA

(1929–2001)

1.

No act of will or Psychic Hotline cant
can raise you from the "utility urn"
I bought you in from Jern's Crematorium
last week. You're done, Mom, and you shan't
correct my English, nor nothing rail nor rant
against forever more. No high-dudgeon
antics can stir the pot. Not even Nieman
Marcus on credit card can make you less than spent.
Farewell to the 12 Minton place settings
you never used, and to the Stickley bed
big as a Roman bath—to the nightshade
and St. John's Wort, masseuse, bed-wettings,
panic calls, blindness—all that pricey dread—
and those who promised love that never came.

2.

You were of course the damaged princess, downed
at seven by the osteomyelitis
in your forehead—surgery, leeches,
one eyelid frozen, headaches that would pound
and pound until you saw yourself as drowned
and then redeemed in your own helplessness.
Great doctors mumbled over you like priests
until the divorce lawyers came and found
your miscarrying mother drug addicted,
your rich daddy a secret queer and crazy.
The baffled judge at last left you to choose.
You were just 10. Your breathing grew constricted
and the courtroom walls leaned in. You told me
how the strange tears splashed on your new red shoes.

3.

And so you chose the mother you would hate
by 17, who stole your friends and lied
and put on airs, while the new poverty tied
you to yourself like a bad smell. Late
to work one morning in the Gulf Coast heat
after a six mile walk, you were mortified
to find deodorant on your desk, tied
up with a little ribbon of pure hate.
That was the day, perhaps, you swore off sweat.
Powdered, perfumed, your beauty cool as ice,
you wore a long red coat, stiletto heels.
When, like soft wind, you tucked me in at night
and whisked away into a world of eyes
and mouths and random men, I felt your steel.

4.

I hear your sniff of violated privacy
as my man's hands riffle the soft innards
of your long bureaus—folded, layered,
immaculate, lush femininity,
but not quite lacy—wombs of secrecy
that hold old letters in frayed ribbons, half-heard
snatches of conversation like the words
of little girls whose coy hypocrisy
you loathed. Was it your father's shortness made
you crave tall men, with timbre in their voices,
who glowered down at me like men on stilts.
Was it just irony the man you married
stood only five foot six and favored boys.
Still I hear the venom of your hissing silks.

5.

Jarvis, Elizabeth Alice, your great
grandmother, slips from a bottom drawer,
faded but lovely as a long-pressed flower,
at perhaps 17. I contemplate
her unstrung collar. She was maybe late
to come in for the photo session hour,
her hair windblown, a breathless now or
never slight parting of the lips. Her fate
was to become an itinerant schoolmarm,
revered for high intelligence and wit,
who married a young minister and raised
three daughters of a certain bearing, charm,
humor and piety. What doesn't quite fit
the story, though, are her eyes—wild, slightly crazed.

6.

What tamed that wild gaze that did not tame yours—
the cold Michigan farm?—anxieties
by candlelight?—the sleepless ministries
to endless household needs? From bottom drawers
they all come tumbling out, the ancestor
church ladies. Your grandmother's diaries,
chock full of weather's cheery godliness,
tell nothing of herself, only her prayers
to better serve. They warmed the glittering ice
of those heartbreaking farms that made you cringe,
if family jottings be believed. White haired,
bleak boned daughters of the mad-eyed Alice,
they show up faded at the faded edges
of family picnics—wistful, shyly proud.

7.

Your existential loathing of the family
tree came early. One minister seduced
proved quite enough. Even old "Elder" Brewster
of the Mayflower hung there in the leafy
branches your mother grew like Blake's Poison Tree.
Its roots were Charlemagne and Robert Bruce,
the Black Douglas and John of Gaunt. No half-truth
was squandered in her quest for ancestry
of might and merit. You were the poor daughter
who'd never measure up to that high-flown bunk
and didn't try. You sang your own mantra.
You were no Mary Ann, let alone "Junior."
You were no pious chip off the old stump.
You changed your name to Alexandra.

8.

Not the carpool mother who sang I Like
Ike songs. Not the girl wounded by her father
who could not say no but not quite yes either.
Not she who made little me one May night
with a blond Mick prize-fighter without quite
conceiving what went on in the weeds there.
Not the petulant, angry daughter,
or even the bad mother or bad wife.
You wanted to exist uncategorically.
You wanted to be an original
created in the diamond moment. Not
for you the pain of being only
one woman. You desired to be impossible,
and stirred and stirred and stirred and stirred the pot.

9.

You loathed your mother's wheeler-dealer lies.
She worried you could *be* but could not do—
and always two stories of what was true—
yours and hers, hers and yours in perfect symmetry—
her outward quest, your inward journey
clashing like cymbals. Both your winds could woo
me. I just saw varying shades of blue—
you darker and she lighter, but the same sea.
You both loved words, and words kept you apart.
In the same room, I'd feel your grinding wills
like creaking oarlocks, both a little crazy
and both killed off by the same bad heart.
You read Proust. She read me Wordsworth's "Daffodils."
In different climes, you each got called "a lady."

10.

All family wars play out best with three.
"What can we do with Alex, what's anyone
to do with Alex," Grandmother would intone
when I was fourteen and thought life easy.
We'd settle in for a long night's breezy
confession of your sins. Crazy as a loon
sometimes, she had the storyteller's one
virtue—to forge some actuality
just as she forged diplomas that got her work.
You were the poor poet of introverted
glances, who saw not things but in their ideas
that fluttered mothily toward the Absurd.
For you communion lurked behind the words.
After dissecting you, we'd have our *brioche.*

11.

You toyed with me with threats of suicide
that year I turned 11. Even then
I thought you were just putting me on
at least half the time. But of course I cried
and rubbed your back, and in my own way tried
to wrestle down your darkest demons
as if you were my double. And just once
I feared you'd kill me in my sleep—some tired
hotel in Switzerland as I recall.
We'd fought. You had been drinking pretty hard.
But I remember mostly how the lake
was blue as lapis and we were immortal.
The incident left us drifting apart.
We just let it alone for beauty's sake.

12.

With enough money nothing need be real.
You blew through seven hundred thousand,
a grand a month for your group psychic plan
alone. The rest, just baubles of the *haute* genteel—
Cartier clocks, drawers full of identical
designer suits in three sizes, not one
worn—scarves and sweaters numberless as sand,
and so on. Mostly it was pretty dismal
being you those last years, ordering things
through U.P.S. to have a moment's friend
when packages arrived. Your eyes were failing
and liver functions—clear rememberings
of things that had not ever happened.
The sirens in your blood-starved head were wailing.

13.

When it was clear the money had run out,
quite willessly you fell upon your sword,
refusing Laesix that your doctor ordered
and losing him for that. For one coquette
moment you tried to call a quick about
face, change your mind. Nurses were guarded—
it was too late now for that. You looked bored
and drifted back to sleep. And that was that.
You new friend-cosmetician held your hand.
Another startled as she entered your room
and one bright blue eye held her in its death-chill.
There was no code blue or shenanigans.
You'd become bride to yet another groom.
The angry child kicking in your head lay still.

14.

Your portraits we brought home filled several boxes—
from Shirley Temple days to the young Hepburn,
your slightly cocked head and cocked eyebrow turn
the gaze inward, despite the outward glances
at the demanding camera. Long eyelashes
veil the quick bright eye. Something flickers and burns
and smolders out. A certain porcelain
veneer distracts us from your beauty's darkness.
What you held dearest was your inner kingdom.
In most all of the portraits, that shows up.
None of them hold the look I cherish—
that devil-may-care, slightly-over-the-top,
what-the-hell grin. That wink. It all said come
dance, little broody boy, it's all there is.

REMAINS

My son guides me up the long hill
squelching in run-off, along trails
narrow as goat paths through the trees
to show me the strewn bones of a deer
nested in her shed shreds of fur,
almost golden, where some wood spirit
laid her to rest, and the coyotes
and crows stripped her, leaving only
a hoof and furred knuckle intact
among a clutter of collapsed ribs.
He shows me the clean white vertebrae,
the pelvis with its odd eye hole,
the knee still attached with some last rope
of sinew.   This is his find, stumbled on
as he tried his new spring legs in a downhill,
helter-skelter run, and stopped, and stared,
and in his eleven year old mind knew
that this was the stuff of running
undone, something the receding snow
left for him personally, a sign
of winter's weight.   We eye it together.
We go down on our knees to gather pieces
of the witchcraft mystery. The gray trees
around us are also bones that click
and chatter in the wet wind
of almost spring. The brown limpid eyes
are gone. The crumbling gnarl
of spine, once nerved and tremulous,
is now only a train wreck the grass
will hide in a month's time. We feel

the doorway of earth opening.
We feel the thinness of our skins
and the prickling of short hairs rising.
We know what's at the bottom of things,
how soon the mayflies will be dancing
their measured reels of the evening.

INVOCATIONS

My steps slower than I would have imagined
even in summer

who once could not help but run
Crimes I've done myself I would not undo

Cicadas in a tree singing
the dappled 'out there'

the shrill of birdsong

★   ★   ★

Sands of the desert and sun warm me
and I forgive my pederast father
and remember his shy laugh

Spawn of East Texas swamps snakes on the brain
Stink of rot and piney woods loneliness
Bible-belt mom dowsed in lavender

I had an engineer's hat like my grandfather's
high in the sun-flared locomotive squinting into the light

the two of us until the whistle blew
and he was a crouched old man on a hospital inner tube

My father's bones shattered like glass and he died
worse than a dog so I forgave him

remembering his shy laugh glints of gold
in his long old teeth

Two funny stories maybe three and no one knew him
His skull in death an old Ojibwa's

★ ★ ★

At night the familiar hocus pocus of moon and mind
You soft in shadow that other
I know myself by

Come Light warm me
Sit on my grandmother's shoulder
who reads me through measles and chickenpox
bringing the world and New Orleans
in two blue suitcases

Light on the banana tree tallest of grasses
Light in her hazel eyes

★ ★ ★

Salt sand of the desert the long unfolding white of it
Out there I stole my bride from the land of the untouchables
Spirit me away dawn of the cockcrow
Light of my wavering window

★ ★ ★

My one great photograph you naked on a chaise lounge
eight months pregnant sleeping in the sun
light circling your circles
and one long draped arm

Light of the moment and always

★ ★ ★

Our son came out a greased chicken when he was born
and shone in the light of all subsequent Christmases

He seemed too small to take home
I had to learn to hold his head up

Your breasts engorged made you the gaudy
fertility goddess carved on a wooden salad spoon
I remembered from childhood

I gave him his first bath
Danced him heart to heart
Happy on the high hill of our summer

★ ★ ★

And happily I am already dead in a book somewhere
but in the dark closed pages or the light of a window
I don't know

To think I was ever a blank page
a tabula rasa a salt flat
a star

Hold the light at the window I am coming
though my knees ache

★ ★ ★

I have always enjoyed near the Equator
how sun maps a face
though I live in the snow

I was young in the sun of tennis courts
Pure form and goat mind
fencing the air

before the flat-light green-haze of hospitals
moon men in surgeries
Mother a mirage in the midnight
arriving from Rome

Stars of Paris outside my window
the girl I held in the dark for 13 years
against my loneliness
swims in the sun of the Pacific now
or is dead

     ★ ★ ★

I made love on a red cliff over the Mediterranean
at midnight in the cove of Los Pinos
to a woman from another language
beautiful as a mermaid
and hairy as a 23 year old
I was young dumb in a hurry
No star touched my soul

     ★ ★ ★

When I think of light I think of salt flats or snow
though its jewels in the leaves are delectable
and fire your black hair

All these summers I've watched you garden our gold hill
Your hillocks not bad Old Woman
raised like prayer

Names of flowers elude me unless I look them up
Is it the desert in me or a dark mind
that cannot name these belles of light'

My first garden was elephant ears and banana trees
and blunt nosed tortoises I kissed on their blunt noses
mossy bricks of the patio
a slight breeze I still recall
on my heat-rashed two-year-old naked buttocks

At three and a ward of the Church
I wanted to bathe with the Deacon's
13 year old daughter Mary Katherine
because I liked her pubic hair
how it swirled in the warm water
One or two baths and everyone thought better of it
From then on it was Morgan or Hank

And still my life seems strange
I think my lake the Danube sometimes
or remember the pale lime-thick turquoise of the Karoon River
an eel under my left foot
in a shock of wonder

Salt flats and snow and the gardens between

★   ★   ★

Wherever it was light wanted to go
I said Yo Dis here is America
Let's do-si-do
Dat old Walt Whitman he big he kind
but boring

Which tribe am I

The twang the drawl the Yankee clipper
Which thrum of weathers
Which codes and netherworlds
Which beestings on the tongue

Or is the eye my alibi
and crude syntax

⭐   ⭐   ⭐

The eye that travels
sees still waves from airplanes
thunderless beaches

In the border towns
of the dead and nearly dead
comes dawn's bleak windows

The casualties were
entirely justified
say the generals

And all that flat line clarity is light

But what of the gutturals of evening
the festooned flesh and ornamental slang
the topsy-turvy muscles of a million mutabilities
carnal carnivals and carnivores
boardwalk bazaar bodega
heartstrings of the tongue's thrumming

when light of the blood is a kind of light

⭐   ⭐   ⭐

I drummed through the booze jungles of Bangkok

at age 15 door to door whore to whore
till one just 17 took me home to meet the folks
and wash me in the kitchen sink
It was intimate chilling a grim mirror
and in the sickly light of the bare bulb
she was truly beautiful
How much of her may have wished to dance
on my grave I don't know

★ ★ ★

Angels and vaginas the angels are
vaginas says my sculptor friend in his studio
when I find his new seraphim
stock and static

Stepping back I see it
Yes
if thighs had wings surely we could fly

From a dark declivity a few curlings
broadening into fern fronds
and baroque arabesques
a vertical mouth for a trunk
and the tree of life is any man's wife

★ ★ ★

And then there were the horses of the sun
ablaze over the clattering rooftops of the world
or at least Khuzistan with its rock hills
and smugglers' trails
A heartbeat between the knees
A breathing like the very wind
Flying the flags of themselves in their girlish manes

the foolishness of all our fathers in their wild eyes

In a monoprint I bought from a friend
three horses graze in a pasture
that might be cloud
the passionless horses of dream or a far field
closer to me now than the horses of wind and fire
muscle and bone
though I miss their salt scent
the rivers of sweat mapping the veins of their necks

Or maybe my friend's print is a dream of horses
dreaming their pastures dreaming their clouds
dreaming the artist dreaming of horses
whose absence is light
around the dark remembered bodies

*   *   *

When my horse the fastest in all Khuzistan died
I was away at college and knew in an instant
my childhood had ended
I tried writing a poem
but couldn't get the Braille of his skin
under my fingers onto the page
He'd lent me the great thunder of his body
and I had lain on his flanks in his stall while he slept
We loved each other with humor like brothers
On the day of our triumph he had blown by
Star of Persia to win by 20 lengths
He nickered and snorted when he heard my footsteps
and when I did not come for months he died
His life blessed mine as only animals can bless
Sometimes our betrayals are mindless as wind
and a man moves emptier than the child that had been

★ ★ ★

Moon of my mind with your long black hair
Come nearer sit opposite
Let me paint you the girl in the rattan chair
one full breast exposed
one knee drawn up that hides the other
A portrait in shadow but the light of the room

Or now the wise handsome woman Penelope old
whom Odysseus fears taking his eyes off
in his fog of years
The firm cool cheek and coolish eyes
and fires that flicker at night
along her spine

Flesh is not sexy to an old man's eye
until defied by gravity the slightly
slipped buttocks that affirms some pride
the waist loosening its stays
that still has grace
the back that arches that's known some ache
Of course it helps he knew the girl
entwined back in that Ithacan Eden world
neither of them doin nothin
that wouldn't make her mama's hair curl

★ ★ ★

The song of the desert is the song of oases
the white sand and midnight blue
of Persian Miniatures

In college I took the Luscher Color Test

"not a party game" we played
as a party game

The colors you chose showed your balance of mind
the book said and I got four asterisks
which meant not even with psychological counseling
would my mind be right

I saw the cultural bias of course
bright yellow and cool green
being the colors of Switzerland on a nice day

I chose burnt orange and a warm brown
the colors "only refugees" had chosen
the colors of Iranian cliff towns

Third I chose a dark blue
which meant according to the book
 I used sex to block my fears
of various underworlds and my sense of doom

O well
The pipes of Pan play
as the pipes of Pan do

And it was a midnight blue
the color of oases
the cry of loons

★   ★   ★

In a glaze of light
the desert men of the high plateau
have faces like worn shoes
Descendents of Alexander's men

their gazes impassive over wide valleys
their stories as cadenced
as Omar Khayyam

Goats jangling like temple bells
they take tea in a circle
talk with their hands
haggling the prices of horses

I know nothing of their wives
or daughters
shadowy sometimes giggly in the doorways

★ ★ ★

No massing of light on a sundown cliff face
was ever more magical than the changing light
in our son's face
The garden gnome crouching at your side
primed to know name and each thrilling step
of each new planting his voice
of query and awe a small
very silvery bell

His little collie Tommy carved trails
into our deep thickets and taught him the woods
quail raccoon an occasional fox
a big black stray he glowered down
like the wrath of God
He died on one of those trails on a sunny day
at just age 10 with a single yelp
Our son's wail like a knife in the heart
lasted forever

What could I teach him the world

is sometimes like a poem but mostly isn't
Distrust moneymen corporate slogans pompous diction

The larger he grew the smaller I seemed

Now he has sideburns like Jim Bowie
and slouches in the sun where he walks

We hope he'll learn to think

★   ★   ★

I wanted to write a poem
whose first line anticipated its last
a box of inevitability
an inevitable box

But life is not like that
Life is a Bob Dylan song
that might go anywhere
or become mumbly and indecipherable

Tramps train whistles a bad sky

We wait for the refrain
Buzzards are circling the bad sky
Tramps enter the train whistles
and then the far blue mountains

But we have faith
Beauty is also circling we think
We wait for the refrain

★   ★   ★

And there you are again in the garden
after long winter and long years
your sports car body our chiropractor
complains you treat like a truck
your mud wife duds a swatch of black earth
glazing your forehead
radiant
pensive
dreaming garden again out of the squalor
of sticks and mud the sprawled
scrawled skeletons
There's no light I'd rather enter
than this sun on our porch in late March
the bare trees on the far hills rusting with inner fires
the lake ice jagged and scarred
and about to vanish

And we could vanish too Love
become wolves on our ancient hill
our tails still plumed and playful
our eyes still fires

a little blood on the sumac leaves
their wands waving toward a new autumn

MARY

(1901-1991)

In that city of black iron lace and Gullah talk,
sin sashaying in shadow, I see you walk
down Pirate's Alley, the quick click of your heels
too Episcopal for the tolling of St. Louis's twelve-tongued bells—
a tea rose in a carnival of azaleas—
white-gloved, sky blue, crisp as your forbearers of East Anglia
yet frankly forgiven in the not quite sultry air
of Easter, taken in by the wide river-mouth patois
of slithering shadows on darkened stairs
in just glimpsed courtyards

and swallowed whole in the black rivers of music,
sirening souls, palaces of jazz-joy, the air thick
with spangled night. A slur of voices
and footfalls on the wet-black streets poised
in mid-summer. Bourbon, Decatur, great
boozy names rolled deep in the throat—
a swill of voices
like the night's breeze, tropical, luscious.
And yours in the plush garden of wrought-iron chairs
crackling like a voice on the wireless—
matter-of-fact as a boot sole,
yet fluttering, fluting its thrill
of the just-so.

You were my first mother in that city of flowering nights
and sweating patios. Duplicitous, cunning,
sometimes mad as a hatter,
you undermined your own daughter
to hold me in the tight
niche of your charms—there where Lafitte

strode and Napoleon's death mask
stared ceilingward, I see you flash—
old outlaw in a city of outlaws,
sainted in a city of saints,
"queers," "reprobates." You gave me awe
and madness, a taste for all things stained

and fallen.
You were my New Orleans,
your chasteness the flip-side of the stripper's martyred gaze,
the sagging wistful gays
your courtiers, the wisteria your bloom.
Mary, they called you. Mary of the crossword puzzle and afternoon
tea, Mary of the rocks, Mary of situations,
whose fall from grace—divorced, shunned,
a bastard grandson and a strident, quick-tongued daughter—
was resurrection in a place of flowers

and music, of terraced talk
on the floating hills of passing nights.
I learned to walk,
your hand in my hand, your electric
voice in my ear.
Even over years, your letters came with the same click
and stutter, your "Angel" signature the relic
of some old family joke
I never quite got.

"The Velvet Bulldozer,"
your doctors whispered near your death.
Your shingles punished you for years,
your retinas detached, your hearing failed.
Only your mind kept ticking in its queer act of will.
In the end, you were vituperative and genteel
as any southern belle. Nurses scuttled.

Doctors deferred. But even their regard
could not hold you forever.
You died with a small sigh—

white in a whited field.

LAMENTATIONS

Lament 1

I sat on the edge of my bed and I wailed and I wept
and I wanted to be empty as wind
and avoid all this old man dying shit
all this piecemeal dissolution humiliation
I wanted to rise like the Phoenix like the sun
and be new in the morning like the sun
I wanted to be 56 forever everything still
almost possible you like a mirage
just ahead within reach a rainbow's
shimmering I wanted to walk in
content in my fate to be walking still walking
the ache in my knees both telling and reassuring
and you in the paper tiara from the party
Queen May aswirl in the ribbons of mock death
and resurrection and I knew making love
 to you would make me whole through the universe
and everything else the denouement the terrible denouement
weeping and keening holding the rags the bitter rags
and then I was empty as wind and quiet

Lament 2

I went to the place of the poem but it was small
and dark and smelled like the ancient dens of foxes
Time kept coming back to scratch at the door
Old words littered the walls as if to keep the damp out
Someone had lit a fire but the ashes were cold
and the spiders were everywhere
And there was such sadness in the spaces between words
so much nothingness in the everything they said
Why fear the nothingness but we do
How fear the meaninglessness which we are
Here is my voice hang it on a tree
Here is my shoe which remembers me
And beautiful were your black diamonds
like the beauty of the sea at night
the points and spires and breezes of the night
where you passed and I followed and the words went out
and I vanished

Lament 3

I wanted to steal the last word from Death I suppose
and the silkiest of thefts are the poems of moonlight
poems of the sea and vast deserts their premonitions
And yet the Angel of Death is all kindness we're told
leading us out into moonlight through cracks in the clouds
had we known had we listened as the terrible talons
of pain and undoing let go
                                      let us pray let us hope
the last ravening moments no end of consciousness
but a beginning
                        let us hope let us pray
though your buttocks domes against my limp gizmo
are all I need tonight to shore me home

Lament 4

How shall I say goodbye to myself poor
Charles Bon in his New Orleans and his emptiness
his decadence and charm and poisonous knowledge
who yet found you beyond all luckiness or fate
Goodbye to the heart hurt by its own betrayals
the mind full of inconsequence and error
a voice too full of itself
knickknacks and charms and the color blue
the silent cries of trees and the lake's sheen
and the numberless leaves haunting the numbered days
The man of the hour is the skeleton in the sombrero
who lies down in the curves of the voluptuous senorita
to a clatter of bedpans in the wings and the cackling of the damned
I sang you the songs of your fiery bones
and the soft opening flower of a dying kiss
Farewell to the grief of days and the holy smell of roses
your face knees voice like water
thighs like snow and eyes full of sky
Your laugh startled me so so so long ago
My will such as it is I give to clouds and to dreaming
my bones to the cathedrals of sand
to the pottery shards of lost places
my eyes to the vulture who resembles me
my wishes to wind and my loneliness
to thousand year old trees and the deserts of desire
I loved you in the simplest of ways my girl
and this is my poem which has no ending

Lament 5

I can imagine the loneliness of widows unraveling
unwelcoming days and old men in shut rooms
measuring their meds losing their minds dates names
If only vanishing were easy an old movie maybe
the corny deathbed speech the melodrama
each bedside mourner a cameo and case study
You see in it the eyes the soul speaking eye
to eye for the last time drinking the last horizon
And the faces strange and the rooms we wake in
with a start the floor moving and the windows dark
are no more ours than the clouds are or the voices of children
Is it the book misplaced that makes me weep
or tortured animals slaughtered children rape
by bayonet or any gone world's going
My grandmother kept a book 85 years pressing
a four-leaf clover given by a friend when they were five
Isn't that worth more than walking on the moon
but nothing stays still straight or in place
but the mute dignity of bones
bones without memory bones without song
So let us go under the hill and over the sky
and let us be bones together

ANCIENT MUSIC

All-ee   All-ee   In   Come   Free

All-ee   All-ee   Outs   In   Free

Ollie   Ollie   Oxen   Free

Ourselves our secrets released from hairy shadows Mother trees
we came bewitched by stars and insect scratchings
We were ghosts made of black mist
We were silent as stones
We had no faces
loud hearts
We felt steely and cruel
like Greeks on a night raid
We came floating like fireflies
toward a language only half our own
Our fathers smelled like Scotch
our mothers like strange flowers
We came lightly padding on our dark animal souls
who knew vanishing was an art
and returning was easy

All-ee All-ee in come free
All-ee All-ee outs in free
Ollie Ollie oxen free

DUST AND A GOOD WIND

(after the photographs of Dorothea Lange)

A lion does not write a book, nor does the weather erect a monument where the pride of a woman was broken for want of a pair of shoes, or where a man worked five years in vain to build a home and gave it up, bankrupt and whipped...or where the wife went insane from sheer monotony and blasted hope.

J. Russell Smith, *North America*. 1925
As recorded in Dorothea Lange's notes.

SIX TENANT FARMERS, WITHOUT FARMS, HARDMAN COUNTY, TEXAS. 1938

Dust
and a good wind
will move mountains.

But these are not mountains,
only men. Each stands
with his own hat in his own pose,

and each stares into the blind eye of the camera
with almost the indifference
with which the blind sun stares. Their lives

have come to this. What moves on the horizon
no longer moves them. Like the dust storm's
gray aftermath, they are a stunned stillness

where the wind has been.
                        A dust storm begins
with a single gray particle, dislodged into wind
and looking for home. All heat and hunger,

it owns nothing and so has nothing to give.

What stands in the wind it demolishes.

What it has picked clean it leaves for the living.

WOMEN OF THE HIGH PLAINS, TEXAS PANHANDLE. 1938

She stands, her long bones dark against the sky,
one hand on neck, the other pressed to her brow,
and she is laughing, as though out of nowhere
something had just dawned, as though somehow
something besides wind had passed through here
on its way to the mountains.
      Listen:
out here the strained hollow faces of summer
grow stranger in winter, the moth-clouds get eaten
by bats from the north, and the long faces of worry
become the low eyeless dwellings of the horizon,
some small smoke rising from the chimneys.
        Listen:
no one alive shall ever hear this laugh, or see
a woman in a flour sack with the posture of a heron
laugh like a child.
     Behind her the bleak plain
lies echoless, where even the bird-call of her bones
shall die
    under the bright clear rain of the million stars.

DAMAGED CHILD, SHACKTOWN, ELM GROVE, OKLAHOMA. 1936

The left eye
is an empty socket. A black stare
into blackness. Behind it: the gray brain that dreams
die back to, like a road map
found on the back seat
of an abandoned car. Shacktown, Elm Grove,
Oklahoma, a place
no one visits, a town that lives
on the rumor of rain.

The smile
is the Mona Lisa's, a vagueness
untouched by vagueness: if one can imagine that
of a half-wit child of eight
who stands in front of four pieces
of dark sheet-metal
that make up the side of a house a child
might throw rocks against
to make thunder.

I once planned
a trip to Nova Scotia, where distance
is decorative. Lakes, rivers: a gentle apportionment
of parts. Four months
went into the planning. It ended
by the side of a road
in a ditch, where a dead dog
grinned and glistened
in the rain.

I carry

a child somewhere in the dark
of my brain. A dead child. She reminds me
of the future. I give her names.
The names change. Today she stands
in front of four pieces of dark sheet-metal
and almost smiles. It is her birthday.
She has just turned eight.
Her one rag

is held together at her right shoulder
by a small knot that is almost a bow.

CHILD AND HER MOTHER, WAPATO, YAKIMA VALLEY, WASHINGTON. 1939

Her hair is long wet strands of dull black weed.
Her head, heavy with it, is bowed. Her eyes
look toward, but do not see, the ground that lies
like iron at her feet. Her fingers knead
and push the barbed wire fence her body's greed
would fold around. But though the one barb tries
to pierce the flesh, the floral dress despise
its thread, the small belly will not take seed.

Her mother stands behind, hand on hip. She'd
rather she stood elsewhere and not be wise
and know down to her bones that no surprise
will come today, that they will not be freed.
Yet she stands, shades her eyes, mouthing a creed
gone bad, wishing it might be otherwise
than to get up each day to the same skies,
hoping there might be something left to bleed.

But sun has honed their land to bone, and grain
no longer tries to flower. The sky is lead,
the days are long, and nothing in a dream
can change the way their shadows seem to stain
the ground, or make them go, or how the dead
come drifting like the echo of a stream

where no stream flows. So let the body steam
in the long night. Let all the shapes of dread
come welling up in the tired shards of brain
until the eyes of child and mother teem
with murder. No help comes to the dark head.
No black blood's pounding brings the vengeance of rain.

ON THE GREAT PLAINS, NEAR WINNER, SOUTH DAKOTA. 1938

On the Great Plains, near Winner, South Dakota,
winters are long. Philosophy is short.
What goes under snow in November
emerges again in March, sometimes later,
sometimes changed. Life's hard. Daughters
get names like Hope or Faith. Sons
don't get far, or move away
altogether, their letters coming back
full of the emptiness they left with.

And here in the space of what looks like
half a mile, maybe less, three churches stand,
one behind the other, like reflections
of the same church: each painted white,
each with its single black spire
thrust into the northern sky. Nothing else
stands or grows, but the prairie grass
moving away like a whisper.

But distance can be tricky here,
so that the church that stands near the horizon
may be a day's walk, maybe farther. And in deep snow
the situation worsens. Destinations are measured
in yards or feet, sometimes inches. Direction,
too, can be confusing. A man goes
snow-blind quickly in a blizzard, sound
distorts, the mind grows muddled.
                              It is said in the desert
a man never dies of thirst
but he will first see water. Here it is said,
a man never freezes to death
but he can hear the ringing of bells.

WALKING WOUNDED, OAKLAND. 1954

There is a moment, albeit hypothetical,
when something foreign
              passing through something familiar
leaves only a blackness,
        a record of travel.

                      Blood bulges
      and overruns the hole,
and sometimes a scream flaps out
        from the first O
                    of astonishment,
the face gathering darkness like a hole
        that will never again
                get quite filled in.

The man in this corridor
        is pure darkness,
                  the forest floor,
a black loam you could lie down in
        dreaming of the long rays of sunlight
                that never come.
        It is dream from which no one wakes.

The man in this corridor
        intrudes
                almost
not at all: a black shoulder, a black pant leg,
        a dead foot and thin line of black crutch
                angling
from behind a telephone pole.
                There's no body,
      only darkness reshuffling.

No face, only a meeting of moles
                holding silent parley
                                in an unmarked grave.

A city is closing
                on the man in this photograph. The telephone pole
looks broad as a door, and the blank wall
                that is the whole right side of the picture
                              looms, somehow,
closer.
                It is washed whiter than any scar.

GRAYSON, SAN JOAQUIN VALLEY, CALIFORNIA. 1938

Say, for a moment, there is this building, too broad
or close for the picture, which looms in the picture
like a bad dream, an image pressed
half on the mind's eye, half onto some darkness
just out of reach.   Lines of raw clapboard cross
from frame to frame, while the rooftree, centered,
lets in two triangles of sky: gray, as the building
is gray, but paler, flatter, if anything
more coincidental than the crude structure
that hulks like a bad conscience on a bleak plain
we do not see, but feel, a dull ache of distance
that comes these last miles to lie in the open crawlspace
like a dark stain.   And the building hangs like that,
in air, between earth and sky, darkness and sun,
and rivets the eye like a pale scar.   Or say it is a building
built to be come to, built like the men who built it,
who, if they knew little of heaven, knew what they needed
of wood and iron, that is made wholly
of wood and iron, built like a hobnail boot.
                                                And say
dead center in the picture, a man lies, that the building
surrounds him as though he had dreamed it, as though
he had nailed each board. But say he is only
a gunny sack with ankles, a corpse left in the shade
where the rotting is slower.   Whether church,
or school, or meeting hall, say it is a building
where men came to listen, its floor and benches

full of splinters, the wind through its boards.
a groaning of iron.
                    Or say the possibilities
run out, that it is a building built by men who spoke prose
and died without fanfare.
                    Say there is this silence.

TOQUERVILLE, UTAH. 1953

Whatever it was, it happened here, sometime after rain
in Toquerville. You walked toward a wall, the progress
slow. It leaned toward you, cracking, as if
trying to accommodate to vague shifts of sunlight
or weather. The scorched air crackled
like an old newsreel (in it men drop like flies, rise
up again, salute and fall back). There was the sound
of rain, a little wind; and slowly the wall took on
a blotchy, blood-splattered look: an enemy wall,
greasy with old deceits, muffled cries.
                                        Then the late sun,
sliding into a window pane, reflected a small path
through the forest, though there was no forest,
only the deceptions of sun in late summer
when the roads, even after rain, stay dusty,
haggard, as from men marching.
                                    You arrived,
flagging, unhealthy. You felt somehow
more like your grandfather: weak-eyed, troubled,
a face forever slashed by a pale blur of sunlight
you are always approaching.
                              Even into twilight.
                                              Turn now
and face this camera full face, the wall
behind you. Remember the evidence,
your grandfather's face: starched, formal.
Remember the patched plaster of faces,
it is all you will ever have to remember.
Remember when the pieces come together
in the cold porcelain of your mind's eye,
it will be someone else's grandfather
who stares out, bland and unblemished,

wearing your face. You will be gone then.
It will be sometime after rain in Toquerville.

MAN STEPPING FROM CURB. 1956

This blind black stepping
into gray this gathering
of light around dark
edges this hanging headless
weightless this hungering
for loose hair and wide
thighs this too taut
skin in too slack
air this hope despair this
running through fingers stone
in the hand empty waking hanged
man thief this gathering
of night dispersement
of stars this flapping
in the breeze this anger
this loneliness this wide
emptiness falling into
stars ether this rise
again into ossified
earth this walking waking
dark angel hanging...

Moon forever rising.
Sun forever falling.
Reflect.   Reflect.

About the Author

Michael Jennings is the author of six previous books of poems, including the collector's item *The Hardman County Sequence* (based on the photographs of Dorothea Lange with a Foreword by W. D. Snodgrass) and *Silky Thefts*, Orchises Press 2007. He is also an internationally recognized breeder and judge of Siberian Huskies, and the author of three books on the breed. He was born in the French Quarter of New Orleans, grew up in east Texas and the deserts of southwestern Iran, graduated from the University of Pennsylvania, and was a Fellow in Creative Writing at Syracuse University. He lives with his wife, poet Suzanne Shane, and their dog pack on a hill overlooking Otisco Lake in Upstate New York.